JOURNEY TO
INVESTIGATING PRI

MAPS
THROUGHOUT AMERICAN HISTORY

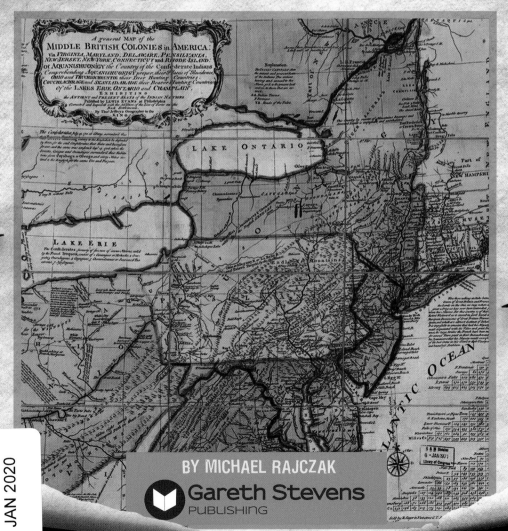

BY MICHAEL RAJCZAK

 Gareth Stevens
PUBLISHING

Please visit our website, www.garethstevens.com. For a free color catalog of all our high-quality books, call toll free 1-800-542-2595 or fax 1-877-542-2596.

Cataloging-in-Publication Data

Names: Rajczak, Michael.
Title: Maps throughout American history / Michael Rajczak.
Description: New York : Gareth Stevens Publishing, 2020. | Series: Journey to the past: investigating primary sources| Includes glossary and index.
Identifiers: ISBN 9781538240427 (pbk.) | ISBN 9781538240441 (library bound) | ISBN 9781538240434 (6 pack)
Subjects: LCSH: Cartography--History--Juvenile literature. | Maps--Juvenile literature. | Voyages and travels--Juvenile literature.
Classification: LCC GA105.6 R335 2020 | DDC 912--dc23

First Edition

Published in 2020 by
Gareth Stevens Publishing
111 East 14th Street, Suite 349
New York, NY 10003

Copyright © 2020 Gareth Stevens Publishing

Designer: Katelyn E. Reynolds
Editor: Jill Keppeler

Photo credits: Cover, pp. 1, 7 (bottom), 9 (both), 11 (top), 13 (top), 17 (both), 19 (bottom), 21 (top), 23 (bottom) courtesy of the Library of Congress; cover, pp. 1-32 (wood background) Miro Novak/Shutterstock.com; cover, pp. 1-32 (old paper) Andrey_Kuzmin/Shutterstock.com; p. 5 sevenMaps7/Shutterstock.com; pp. 7 (top), 15 Rainer Lesniewski/Shutterstock.com; p. 11 (bottom) Gwillhickers/Wikipedia.org; p. 13 (bottom) Library and Archives Canada, e002418569/Attribution 2.0 Generic (CC BY 2.0); p. 21 (bottom) David Pollack/Corbis via Getty Images; p. 23 (top) NOAA/ https://www.ncdc.noaa.gov/temp-and-precip/drought/historical-palmers/ psi/193407-193407; p. 25 (both) courtesy of NASA; p. 27 (map) DNetromphotos/ Shutterstock.com; p. 27 (Hillary Clinton) Evan El-Amin/Shutterstock.com; p. 27 (Donald Trump) Christopher Halloran/Shutterstock.com; p. 29 Jaap Arriens/ NurPhoto via Getty Images.

Printed in the United States of America

CPSIA compliance information: Batch #CS19GS: For further information contact Gareth Stevens, New York, New York at 1-800-542-2595.

CONTENTS

WORDS IN THE GLOSSARY APPEAR IN **BOLD** TYPE
THE FIRST TIME THEY ARE USED IN THE TEXT.

WHAT IS A PRIMARY SOURCE?

When something happens, the best **descriptions** of the event will probably be from eyewitnesses. These are people who were there and saw firsthand what happened. Primary sources are sources created by witnesses close to the time of the event. They provide the most **accurate** accounts. Pictures, videos, and written **documents** can be primary sources.

When news reporters collect information about events, they interview people who were there. Those people's stories are primary sources. **Artifacts** may also be primary sources. For example, if you see a tool created long ago, you may imagine how someone once used it. This could help you understand what life was like then. Looking at an old picture can show you what people dressed like or how they traveled. Maps can also be good primary sources.

ANALYZE IT!

THINK ABOUT MAPS YOU SEE EVERY DAY. WHAT DO THEY SHOW?

MAPS AS
PRIMARY SOURCES

MAPS MAY SHOW MANY DIFFERENT THINGS. THEY OFTEN HAVE SYMBOLS. FOR EXAMPLE, A STAR MAY REPRESENT A CAPITAL CITY. SOME MAPS SHOW THE SIZE AND SHAPE OF BODIES OF WATER, STATES, AND COUNTRIES. MAPS MAY USE COLOR TO SHOW MOUNTAINS, WATER, OR STREETS. WHAT A MAP SHOWS—OR DOESN'T SHOW—MAY GIVE YOU INFORMATION ON WHAT PEOPLE THOUGHT AND KNEW WHEN THAT MAP WAS MADE.

THE STAR FOR ALBANY ON THIS MAP MEANS THAT IT'S THE CAPITAL OF NEW YORK STATE. THE DIFFERENT-COLORED LINES MARK DIFFERENT TYPES OF ROADS AND HIGHWAYS.

PIECES OF THE UNITED STATES

The map of the United States today is the result of many things that happened in the past. It looks complete and familiar to many people because the country has looked like this for nearly 60 years. However, it didn't always look this way.

One example of the changes is in Florida. Britain controlled the area after the American Revolution. At the time, there was a West Florida and an East Florida. West Florida reached all the way to the Mississippi River. In the early 1800s, US settlers started moving into West Florida. In time, the territory was divided, with the western Florida border at the Perdido River. The rest became part of Mississippi, Alabama, and Louisiana. In 1819, the United States acquired all of Florida.

ANALYZE IT!

LOOK AT A MAP OF THE ORIGINAL 13 COLONIES. WHY DO YOU THINK THE EUROPEANS SETTLING IN NORTH AMERICA SETTLED WHERE THEY DID?

THE ORIGINAL
13 COLONIES

THE UNITED STATES STARTED WITH 13 BRITISH COLONIES IN NORTH AMERICA. MASSACHUSETTS, NEW HAMPSHIRE, CONNECTICUT, RHODE ISLAND, NEW YORK, NEW JERSEY, PENNSYLVANIA, DELAWARE, MARYLAND, VIRGINIA, SOUTH CAROLINA, NORTH CAROLINA, AND GEORGIA WERE CLUSTERED TOGETHER ON THE EAST COAST OF THE CONTINENT, ALL THE WAY TO THE RIGHT WHEN YOU LOOK AT A MAP OF THE UNITED STATES TODAY.

MODERN MAP OF THE UNITED STATES

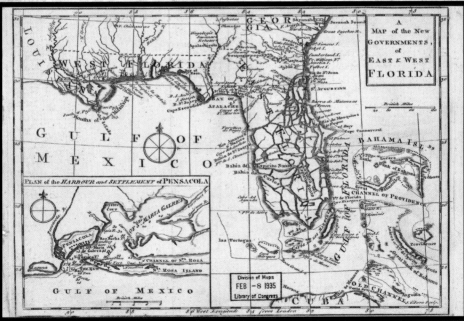

THIS MAP FROM 1763 SHOWS WEST FLORIDA AND EAST FLORIDA. THE RED LINE IS THE PERDIDO RIVER, WHICH IS THE WESTERN BORDER OF THE STATE OF FLORIDA TODAY.

TREATY OF PARIS, 1783

The Proclamation of 1763, issued by Great Britain at the end of the French and Indian War, banned the American colonists from settling on the land west of the Appalachian Mountains. It also required any colonists already living there to leave. Great Britain didn't want another war against Native Americans, and much of that land was Native American territory. The proclamation angered many colonists, who wanted to expand the colonies, and contributed to the anti–British sentiment that eventually became the American Revolution.

After the American Revolution ended, the Treaty of Paris in 1783 gave much of the land between the Appalachian Mountains and the Mississippi River to the new United States. This land, in time, became a number of new states, including Michigan, Ohio, and Illinois.

ANALYZE IT!

WHY DO YOU THINK THE COLONISTS FELT THEY DESERVED THE LAND WEST OF THE APPALACHIAN MOUNTAINS? HOW DO YOU THINK THE NATIVE AMERICANS WHO LIVED THERE FELT ABOUT THAT?

YORKTOWN

THE FINAL MAJOR BATTLE OF THE AMERICAN REVOLUTION TOOK PLACE IN FALL 1781 AT YORKTOWN, VIRGINIA. THE MAP INSERT SHOWS HOW FRENCH AND AMERICAN TROOPS SURROUNDED A BRITISH BASE UNDER THE COMMAND OF GENERAL CHARLES CORNWALLIS. WITH THE FRENCH NAVAL FLEET ARRIVING TO CUT OFF ANY CHANCE OF A BRITISH ESCAPE, CORNWALLIS HAD TO SURRENDER. SOON, THE WAR WAS OVER. THE UNITED STATES HAD WON ITS INDEPENDENCE.

SIEGE OF YORKTOWN MAP

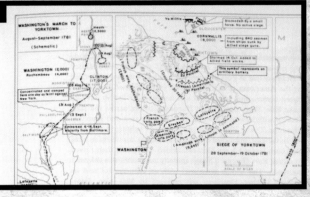

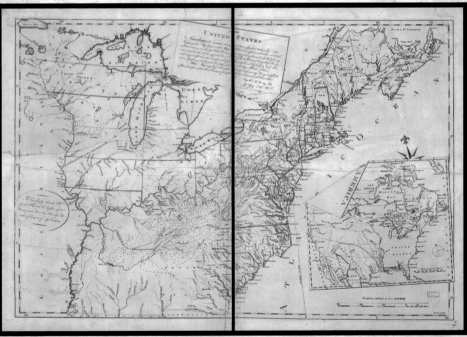

THE FIRST THREE NEW STATES AFTER THE ORIGINAL 13 WERE VERMONT, KENTUCKY, AND TENNESSEE.

THE LOUISIANA PURCHASE

In 1803, the United States wanted to purchase the port of New Orleans at the mouth of the Mississippi River from France. Napoleon, the emperor of France, surprised US representatives by offering them the entire Louisiana Territory for $15 million. This huge amount of land doubled the size of the young United States. However, most of Louisiana had never been explored or mapped.

President Thomas Jefferson had long been interested in what lay between the Mississippi River and the Pacific Ocean. He envisioned a river route up the Missouri River, over a narrow mountain ridge, and onward all the way to the ocean. However, the best available maps didn't provide details. Jefferson directed Meriwether Lewis and William Clark to lead an expedition into the territory.

ANALYZE IT!

COUNTRIES SOMETIMES DISAGREE OVER BORDERS. WHAT ARE SOME WAYS YOU CAN THINK OF TO SETTLE THESE DISAGREEMENTS?

WHERE IS THE END?

IMAGINE PURCHASING 828,000 SQUARE MILES (2.14 MILLION SQ. KM) OF LAND AND NOT KNOWING THE NORTHERN OR WESTERN BOUNDARIES. NO ONE QUITE KNEW JUST WHERE THE LOUISIANA TERRITORY ENDED. AT ONE TIME, SPAIN, BRITAIN, RUSSIA, AND THE UNITED STATES ALL CLAIMED LAND IN THE NORTHWEST, CALLED THE OREGON TERRITORY. BECAUSE LEWIS AND CLARK HAD REACHED THE PACIFIC OCEAN THERE, THE UNITED STATES CLAIMED IT WAS PART OF LOUISIANA.

1802 MAP

1814 MAP

ON THIS MAP FROM 1814, YOU CAN SEE HOW MUCH DETAIL LEWIS AND CLARK WERE ABLE TO ADD TO THIS SECTION OF THE UNITED STATES.

THE WAR OF 1812

The map to the lower right, from around the time of the War of 1812, gives some **perspective** on the development of the Great Lakes area. You can see the names of many Native American groups on the map. This was their land and their territory.

The War of 1812 between the British and the United States included many Native American groups. Many Native Americans sided with the British, fighting to stop the US takeover and settlement of their lands. One key leader was Shawnee chief Tecumseh, who worked to unite many native tribes against the United States. His death and the deaths of many other Native Americans in the war meant the United States could take more Native American lands afterward.

ANALYZE IT!

HOW DO YOU THINK THE BRITISH FELT WHEN THEY SAW THE AMERICAN FLAG FLYING OVER FORT MCHENRY? HOW DO YOU THINK AMERICAN WATCHERS FELT?

FORT MCHENRY
PROTECTS BALTIMORE

DURING THE WAR OF 1812, THE STAR-SHAPED FORT MCHENRY PROTECTED THE SEA APPROACH TO BALTIMORE. YOU CAN LOCATE THE FORT ON THE MAP BELOW BY FINDING THE SMALL STAR NEAR THE LOWER RIGHT. NOTICE THAT THE FORT'S LOCATION IS IDEAL, OUT ON A **PENINSULA**. TO ATTACK BALTIMORE, THE BRITISH NAVY WOULD HAVE TO GET PAST FORT MCHENRY. THE BRITISH SHIPS RAINED DOWN CANNON FIRE, BUT EARLY THE NEXT MORNING, THERE WAS STILL A HUGE AMERICAN FLAG FLYING OVER THE FORT.

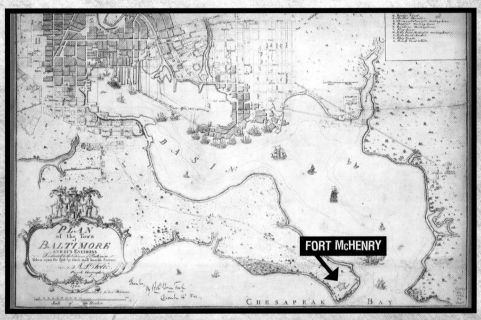

FORT McHENRY

1813 MAP OF THE GREAT LAKES

THE WAR OF 1812 AND THE TREATY THAT ENDED IT DID MUCH DAMAGE TO THE NATIVE AMERICAN NATIONS OF NORTH AMERICA.

ANNEXATION OF
TEXAS

When American settlers and others in Texas won their independence from Mexico in 1836, they asked to become part of the United States. Some members of Congress didn't approve because Texas allowed slavery. Also, some people worried that **annexing** Texas might cause a war with Mexico. It took nine years before the United States did annex Texas, which became the 28th state in December 1845.

However, Mexico and the United States couldn't agree on where the border of the new state was. Mexico said the Nueces River was the border. The United States said the border was the Rio Grande. When American troops occupied the land between the two rivers, Mexican troops attacked. This was the start of the Mexican–American War, which lasted from 1846 to 1848.

ANALYZE IT!

WHY DO YOU THINK SO MANY BORDERS ARE SET AT RIVERS OR MOUNTAINS?

A BIG ADDITION

THE 1848 TREATY OF GUADALUPE HIDALGO ENDED THE MEXICAN–AMERICAN WAR. MEXICO GAVE THE UNITED STATES MORE THAN 525,000 SQUARE MILES (1.4 MILLION SQ. KM) OF LAND. THIS ADDITION TO THE UNITED STATES BECAME ALL OR PART OF THE STATES OF ARIZONA, CALIFORNIA, COLORADO, NEVADA, NEW MEXICO, TEXAS, AND UTAH. THE NEW BORDER BETWEEN THE TWO NATIONS HAD TO BE CAREFULLY ESTABLISHED. THE BORDER IS NEARLY 2,000 MILES (3,218.7 KM) LONG.

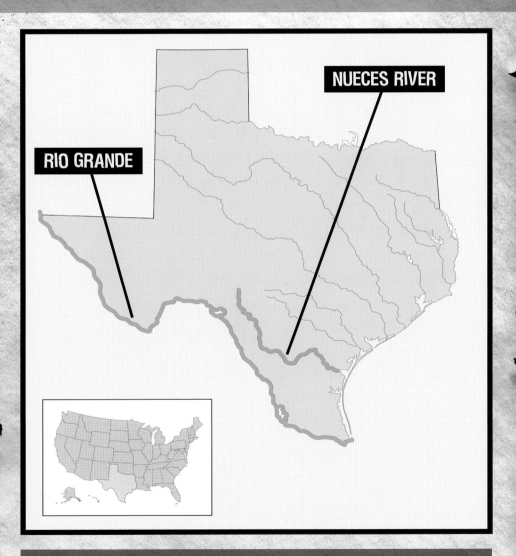

NUECES RIVER

RIO GRANDE

IN 1846, US PRESIDENT JAMES POLK SENT GENERAL ZACHARY TAYLOR AND US TROOPS TO OCCUPY THE LAND BETWEEN THE NUECES RIVER AND THE RIO GRANDE. HE THEN ASKED CONGRESS TO DECLARE WAR WHEN MEXICAN TROOPS ATTACKED.

THE CIVIL WAR

Maps can be used to tell stories or explain events. A map of the southern United States in 1864 is shown to the lower right. This map, from near the end of the American Civil War, shows that the Union had taken over the Mississippi River. This split the remaining **Confederate** states into two parts. The western part was on the other side of the Mississippi River. At the time, few bridges crossed the river.

Because the Union controlled that river, the western part of the Confederacy was cut off from the eastern part. The area of lighter gray on the map is Confederate land that had been captured by the Union. The darker gray areas show what is left of Confederate territory. The Union was well on its way to winning the Civil War.

ANALYZE IT!

HOW DO YOU THINK MAPS HELP GENERALS AND LEADERS PLAN BATTLES? WHY IS IT IMPORTANT TO KNOW THE AREA?

SCOTT'S GREAT SNAKE

"SCOTT'S GREAT SNAKE" REFERS TO UNION GENERAL WINFIELD SCOTT'S PLAN TO DEFEAT THE CONFEDERATE STATES. SOME PEOPLE CALLED IT THE "ANACONDA PLAN," AFTER A SNAKE THAT SQUEEZES ITS PREY TO DEATH. THE PLAN INCLUDED BLOCKING THE SOUTH FROM TRADE AND GAINING CONTROL OF THE MISSISSIPPI RIVER. MANY PEOPLE DIDN'T LIKE SCOTT'S PLAN BECAUSE THEY DIDN'T THINK IT WAS QUICK ENOUGH. HOWEVER, THE WAR LASTED LONGER THAN PEOPLE ORIGINALLY THOUGHT IT WOULD.

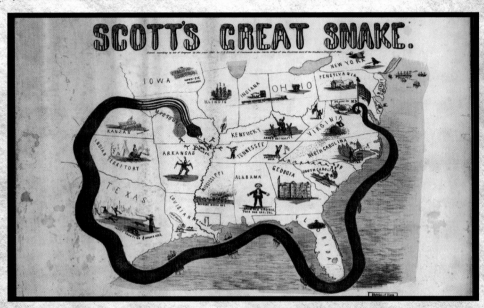

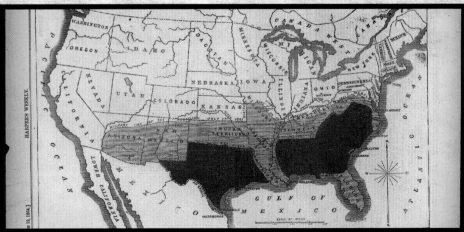

THE CIVIL WAR STARTED IN APRIL 1861 AND ENDED IN MID-1865. HUNDREDS OF THOUSANDS OF PEOPLE DIED IN THE WAR.

THE TRANSCONTINENTAL RAILROAD

Before the railroads, most people worked and traded close to where they lived. Starting in 1869, the first transcontinental, or across the continent, railroads connected many existing railroads in the eastern United States with the Pacific coast. The railroads opened whole new markets for crops, livestock, and manufactured goods. Where cattle trails crossed railroad lines, towns sprang up. When a north-south railroad met an east-west railroad, a new city was often created.

Two of the cities affected by the railroads were Cheyenne, Wyoming, and Denver, Colorado. Cheyenne began as a railroad depot. After the railroads arrived in the West in 1870, the mining settlement of Denver grew from fewer than 5,000 people to more than 100,000 in just 20 years.

ANALYZE IT!

WHAT KINDS OF CHANGES DO YOU THINK HAPPENED IN SAN FRANCISCO AFTER THE TRANSCONTINENTAL RAILROAD WAS COMPLETED?

CALIFORNIA

THE TRANSCONTINENTAL RAILROAD'S WESTERN END WAS IN SAN FRANCISCO. THIS ALLOWED EASIER TRAVEL TO THE WEST FOR PEOPLE WHO WERE INTERESTED IN LOOKING FOR GOLD OR STARTING BUSINESSES. MANY ASIAN **IMMIGRANTS** CAME TO NORTH AMERICA TO BUILD THE RAILROAD. THEY TRANSFORMED THE RICH VALLEYS OF CALIFORNIA INTO SUCCESSFUL FARMLAND. THE RAILROAD TRANSPORTED CROPS TO THE EAST.

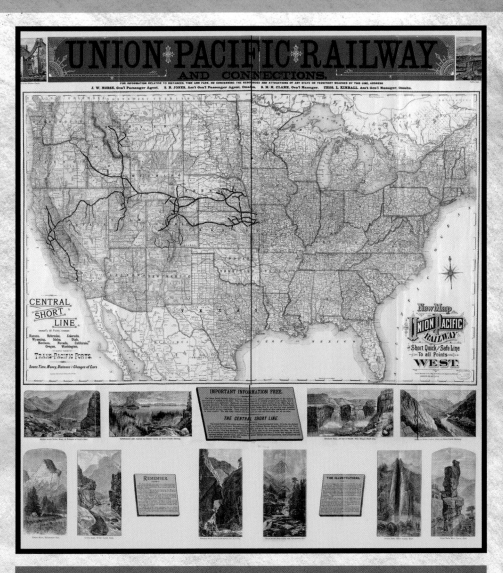

BEFORE THE TRANSCONTINENTAL RAILROAD, IT TOOK ABOUT SIX MONTHS TO TRAVEL FROM NEW YORK TO SAN FRANCISCO. ON THE RAILROAD, IT TOOK A WEEK AND COST FAR LESS.

PANAMA CANAL

Before a canal connected the Atlantic and Pacific Oceans, ships leaving New York had to travel 12,000 miles (19,312.1 km) around South America to reach California. In the late 1800s, the United States was growing and developing. Many people wanted to travel to the West Coast.

After Panama won its independence from Colombia, the new country and the United States reached an agreement in 1903 to allow the United States to build a canal that crossed the **Isthmus** of Panama. This was a huge job. The canal cost $400 million and took 10 years to complete, opening in 1914. Thanks to the canal, the trip from New York to California was now only 4,000 miles (6,437.4 km), took far less time, and cost much less.

ANALYZE IT!

IF YOU COULD BUILD A SECOND CANAL BETWEEN THE PACIFIC AND ATLANTIC OCEANS, WHERE WOULD BE THE BEST PLACE TO PUT IT?

A HUMAN COST

THE PANAMA CANAL IS ABOUT 40 MILES (64.4 KM) LONG.
IT WAS A HUGE ENGINEERING FEAT. WORKERS HAD TO CUT
THEIR WAY THROUGH THE EARTH USING STEAM SHOVELS AND OTHER
TOOLS AND MACHINES. THEY DEALT WITH LANDSLIDES AND EXPLOSIVE
ACCIDENTS. MORE THAN 56,000 PEOPLE WORKED ON THE PROJECT. MORE
THAN 5,600 WORKERS DIED FROM ACCIDENTS AND DISEASES WHILE BUILDING
THE CANAL.

THIS MAP WAS A COMMON PURCHASE FOR TOURISTS WHO VISITED THE CANAL ZONE IN
PANAMA. THE CANAL WAS A HUGE UNDERTAKING AND PEOPLE WERE AMAZED BY IT.

THE DUST BOWL

The Great Plains area of the United States contains vast grasslands. Many free-roaming cattle and buffalo once lived there. Many farmers and ranchers settled this area beginning in the late 1800s. Farmers plowed the land to plant wheat, especially as World War I started in the early 1900s. This damaged the land as the natural grasses were destroyed.

Then, in the early 1930s, a period of extreme **drought** made things even worse. Windstorms blew the dry, exposed soil away, ruining farms and ranch land. The storms carried the dry soil as far as the East Coast. Skies darkened with flying dirt for days at a time. At the same time, the **Great Depression** hit the United States. Many farmers could not pay their bills and lost their farms and homes.

ANALYZE IT!

THE WORST OF THE DUST STORMS TOOK PLACE ON APRIL 14, 1935. IT WAS CALLED "BLACK SUNDAY" BECAUSE THE SKY TURNED BLACK. CAN YOU IMAGINE THAT?

LEAVING THE PLAINS

DURING THE 1930S, ABOUT 2.5 MILLION PEOPLE LEFT THE GREAT PLAINS. MANY LEFT TO TRY TO BUILD A NEW LIFE IN CALIFORNIA AND OTHER PLACES NOT AS AFFECTED BY THE DUST STORMS. WITHOUT MONEY, THESE PEOPLE TOOK WHAT JOBS THEY COULD FIND, OFTEN PICKING CROPS. THEY WERE VERY POOR. THIS DUST BOWL **MIGRATION** BECAME A SYMBOL OF POVERTY IN AMERICA.

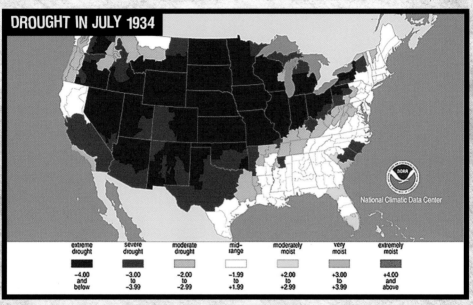

DROUGHT IN JULY 1934

National Climatic Data Center

extreme drought	severe drought	moderate drought	mid-range	moderately moist	very moist	extremely moist
−4.00 and below	−3.00 to −3.99	−2.00 to −2.99	−1.99 to +1.99	+2.00 to +2.99	+3.00 to +3.99	+4.00 and above

THE PHOTO SHOWS A DUST STORM OVER TEXAS IN 1936.

MOON MAPS

Maps don't always show Earth. When the Apollo program started in the 1960s, NASA needed to use maps of the moon to figure out where astronauts could land safely and what they would do. NASA used maps to come up with five possible landing sites that were smooth and had good light, as well as other factors.

Astronauts Neil Armstrong and Edwin "Buzz" Aldrin, who walked on the moon during the Apollo 11 mission in July 1969, collected lunar, or moon, samples; did experiments; and took photos. This was the first time people had stepped on the moon's surface. Over the course of the Apollo missions from 1966 to 1972, 12 astronauts walked on the moon. Some even drove a lunar rover, or vehicle, there!

ANALYZE IT!

WHAT DO YOU THINK WERE SOME OF THE OTHER FACTORS NASA USED TO PICK LANDING SITES FOR THE APOLLO MISSIONS?

MEN ON THE MOON

THE 12 MEN WHO'VE WALKED ON THE MOON ARE NEIL ARMSTRONG, BUZZ ALDRIN, PETE CONRAD, ALAN BEAN, ALAN SHEPARD, EDGAR MITCHELL, DAVID SCOTT, JAMES IRWIN, JOHN YOUNG, CHARLES DUKE, EUGENE CERNAN, AND HARRISON SCHMITT. THAT'S TWO PEOPLE PER MISSION, FROM APOLLO 11 TO APOLLO 17. APOLLO 13 NEVER LANDED ON THE MOON BECAUSE OF AN ACCIDENT. SCOTT AND IRWIN WERE THE FIRST TO DRIVE THE LUNAR ROVER.

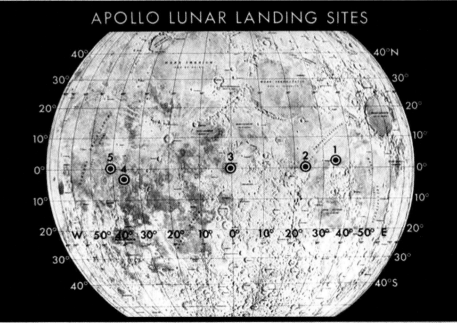

ARMSTRONG AND ALDRIN SPENT TWO AND A HALF HOURS WALKING ON THE MOON'S SURFACE DURING THE APOLLO 11 MISSION.

ELECTORAL MAPS

Many TV news shows, magazines, and newspapers use electoral maps during elections. Often, these maps are color coded. You can learn a great deal about elections by looking at electoral maps. Before an election, you can learn about areas of the country in which a presidential candidate has strong support. Afterward, you can learn the voting results.

On the map to the right showing the results of the 2016 election, you can see that Democratic candidate Hillary Clinton had support in the Northeast, while Republican candidate Donald Trump had support in the South and Midwest. Some maps show how many electoral votes each state has. Electoral votes are based on representation in Congress. While this map looks very red, Clinton received more overall votes than Trump.

ANALYZE IT!

WHY DO YOU THINK CANDIDATES OFTEN VISIT THE STATES WITH THE LARGEST NUMBER OF ELECTORAL VOTES?

STATE ELECTIONS

ELECTORAL MAPS ALSO ARE USED IN STATE ELECTIONS. AN ELECTORAL MAP CAN SHOW YOU MORE ABOUT THE ELECTION OF THE GOVERNOR OF NEW YORK IN 2018. GOVERNOR ANDREW CUOMO WON IN THE STATE'S MAJOR CITIES: NEW YORK, BUFFALO, ROCHESTER, SYRACUSE, AND ALBANY. HOWEVER, HE WON IN ONLY SEVEN OF 62 COUNTIES IN NEW YORK STATE. SINCE MANY MORE PEOPLE LIVE IN NEW YORK'S CITIES, HE EASILY WON REELECTION.

HOW THE USA VOTED IN 2016
THE WINNING MARGIN IN THOUSANDS

DEMOCRATIC CANDIDATE

REPUBLICAN CANDIDATE

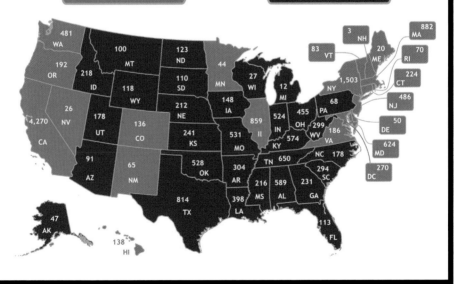

THIS MAP SHOWS THE WINNING MARGIN (IN THE THOUSANDS) IN THE POPULAR VOTE IN EACH STATE IN THE 2016 ELECTION, NOT THE ELECTORAL VOTE.

YOUR TURN TO
EXPLORE

You can use maps to learn more about any place on Earth—and sometimes beyond. If you're going to visit an amusement park, you could use a map of the park to locate rides and attractions. On a map of a vacation resort, you could find all the pools and restaurants.

If you're going somewhere—or if you're just interested in learning about other places—it's good to know that many maps are available on the internet now. Smartphones and computers can run applications that can give you live map updates. You can get warnings about construction and traffic problems. You can get directions. You can see weather alerts. You can even see where other people think the best restaurants are. Maps can be useful and fun!

ANALYZE IT!

IF YOU COULD INVENT A MAP APP, WHAT WOULD YOU CHOOSE TO FOCUS ON?

LOCATION TRACKING

IF YOU'RE LOOKING AT A MAP ON A SMARTPHONE, TABLET, OR ANOTHER COMPUTER, IT MAY HAVE A STAR OR ARROW SHOWING WHERE ON THE MAP YOU ARE. THIS CAN BE BOTH USEFUL AND A LITTLE WEIRD. COMPUTERS OFTEN CAN FIND YOUR LOCATION BY PINGING, OR SIGNALING, **SATELLITES**, INTERNET PROVIDERS, OR OTHER RESOURCES. THERE ARE WAYS TO TURN THIS OFF, HOWEVER.

AS TIME GOES ON, MORE CARS AND OTHER VEHICLES MAY HAVE SCREENS THAT CONNECT TO MAP APPLICATIONS. YOU MIGHT NOT EVEN NEED TO USE A SMARTPHONE!

GLOSSARY

accurate: free from mistakes

annex: to take over an area and make it part of a larger territory

artifact: something made by humans in the past

Confederate: having to do with the Confederate States of America during the American Civil War

description: a statement that tells you how something looks, sounds, etc.

document: a formal piece of writing

drought: a long period of very dry weather

Great Depression: a period of economic troubles with widespread unemployment and poverty (1929–1939)

immigrant: one who comes to a country to settle there

isthmus: a narrow strip of land with sea on either side

migration: the act of migrating, or moving from one place to another for work or another reason

peninsula: a narrow piece of land that extends into water from the mainland

perspective: point of view

satellite: an object that circles Earth in order to collect and send information or aid in communication

FOR MORE INFORMATION

BOOKS

Balkin, Gabrielle. *The 50 States: Activity Book—Maps of the 50 States of the USA.* Wide Eyed Editions, 2016.

Lavagno, Enrico. *Maps of the World: An Illustrated Children's Atlas of Adventure, Culture, and Discovery.* New York: Black Dog & Leventhal, 2018.

National Geographic Society. *National Geographic Kids Beginner's United States Atlas.* Washington, DC: National Geographic, 2016.

WEBSITES

A Territorial History of the United States
www.the-map-as-history.com/timeline/Usa/
This moving timeline showing how and when territory was added to the United States can help you understand why the country looks the way it does today.

USA Map Match
kidsgeo.com/geography-games/usa-map-match/
Find a worksheet to put US states in place on a map as fast as you can!

Explore the World!
kids.nationalgeographic.com/world/
On this National Geographic website, kids can play with an interactive map and learn more about the countries of the world.

Publisher's note to educators and parents: Our editors have carefully reviewed these websites to ensure that they are suitable for students. Many websites change frequently, however, and we cannot guarantee that a site's future contents will continue to meet our high standards of quality and educational value. Be advised that students should be closely supervised whenever they access the Internet.

INDEX